72"

66"

Robert Asafo Williams

March 11, 1989

21st Century Slavery

BY: ROBERT ASAFO WILLIAMS

25 YEARS ENSLAVED:
A PENNSYLVANIA PRISONER'S APPEAL
TO THE PEOPLE FOR FREEDOM

BY: ROBERT ASAFO WILLIAMS

OPEN LETTER TO THE PEOPLE 📝

Dear People,

I am writing this letter to you from the confines of one of Pennsylvania's most dreadful neo plantations, but with an untethered heart and an unchained mind, and in the flesh & spirit of my true Afrikan self and not as the colonial subject my captors wishes me to be; with a solemn meditation that my honorable ancestors will guide my pen - and aid in the escape of these words - smuggling them not only past these cell bars, barbwire fences, gun-towers and state-hired goons, but also the artificial barriers, stigmas & stereotypes constructed by today's slave makers, to maintain their age-old tactics of 'Divide & Conquer', as it pertains to their efforts to cut the modern-day enslaved off from the rest of the world, especially from you, The People.

I am Asafo Chuma Asafo. However, on all government paperwork relevant to my incarceration/enslavement and other state dossier, I am identified by the colonial name: Robert Williams - a name I have openly denounced in favor of the former. I have been held in state captivity for more than 25 years - on a trumped up 2nd degree murder conviction. I was 19 years-old when I was captured, charged and lead away in chains by the modern 'patty rollers' and subjected ever since to one state internment camp after another, where I have pretty much grown up. I never got the chance to experience a 'normal' life, including one of the most fundamental tenets of being human, which is to have children. With the exception of a fist-full of committed family & friends, I have grown accustomed to people bouncing in & out of my life, with no real permanence; a fragmented social circumstance, no doubt, attributable to my protracted captivity.

People, this letter isn't to elicit any undue pity. Nor is it an attempt to paint myself with the brush of a saint. My formative years were honed in the mean streets of Philadelphia, replete with all of their dirty elements. So, much of what the streets say I did, I'll be the first to affirm. In the words & spirit of honorable ancestor Amilcar Cabral. "Mask no difficulties; Claim no easy victories; And tell no lies to The People." So I come to you, The People, with both hands exposed, palms up, with remnants of grit still in the cracks.

But I assure you, I am still in possession of my honor, my integrity and, more importantly, my Afrikan soul.

To the dismay of my captors, I have been redeemed by Malcolm X, Queen Mother Moore, Elijah Muhammad, Sister Marimba Ani, Dr. Amos N. Wilson, Dr. Frances Cress Welsing, Mwalimu Baruti and other warrior-scholars and honorable ancestors.

A lot of what has been said and documented about me, for much of my life, has been scribed by the state's yellow pen - and squeezed between the narrow margins of "official" court documents - padded prison records and ambiguous statistical language, to justify my prolonged captivity - and to dissuade you - The People, from caring. So this letter (and accompanying Appeal) comes to you, The People - in my own words - flaws & all, so you can decide for yourselves what's what.

And while this writing is composed in 'first person', I assure you that I speak for thousands of captured men (and women) whose voices and very existence have been gagged & bound and intentionally misrepresented to the public. But LO! The masses are awaking (globally), to the lies and mischaracterizations of an entire people just to facilitate their collective demise. A people with whom I share a common history, bloodline and struggle.

Throughout the ensuing pages of this small booklet I will be using the identifying term Afrikan interchangably with, but mostly in the place of, 'Black', to identify us in connection to the Land from which we come. There is no such land or nation called 'Black'. The 'K' in Afrikan signifies our unique history of struggle and accumulated experiences here in this western hemisphere and the global diaspora upon our forced removal from our Mother-Land, while maintaining a connection to our cultural core both continental & traditional.

Being uneducated in the conventional or classical sense when I was first captured, I used this time to proactively educate myself, using the autodidact or 'Malcolm X' formula; and having the good fortune to encounter such master teachers as Ministers Alif & Joshua Asadi - Elders Maroon, Jaffer Saidi, Shabaka & Sakin - respectively, among others, within the God-forsaken dungeons of Pennsylvania's most repressive gulags.

In recent years, thanks to the ever-present camera phone and social media, the whole world has witnessed white cops (and other colorful agents of the state) brutalize, demonize/criminalize and outright murder Afrikans and other non-whites all over this country, with impunity. And the spates of popular rebellions in their wake have effectively removed all pretence of 'Serve & Protect', exposing the police apparatus for racist Blue-Blooded fraternity that it is, including its corporate-owned media co-conspirators. And now that the 'Us versus Them' stance taken by the police establishment, and mainstream media, is out in the open, popular resistance is beginning to take shape. The Black Lives Matter movement and countless others are the evidence of this. Moreover, their decentralized postures have thus far proved to be a bit too nimble for the state to just box in and be done with - which shows great potential for it to augment into a full fledge Black Liberation Movement - with its many moving parts contending on the frontiers where we are most under attack. It is to you, the burgeoning critical mass (of People) that I put forth this Appeal.

The political shift from "Lock 'em up and throw-away-the-key" to "Criminal Justice Reform", as it pertains to mass incarceration, is a result of you, The People, taking it to the streets, exposing the 'race-based' contradictions in 'Criminal Just-Us' and the broader hypocrisies of Amerikkkan "democracy". Furthermore, the unprecedented solidarity displayed by thousands of courageous Hunger Strikers throughout California's repressive prison/ plantation system, which spread to other states - even other countries - effectively exposing the true torturous nature of America's prisons, in stark contrast to their foisted mantra of "REHABILITATION"; The massive prisoner strikes in Georgia's wretched prison system back in 2010, and the brave work done by the Free Alabama Movement (FAM) and other prison-based formations were instrumental in bringing global attention to the 'Business' of American-Style mass incarceration.

It is important to also mention the work being done by the HUMAN RIGHTS COALITION in Pennsylvania's prisons along with the DECARCERATE PA collective, the LEGATEE MOVEMENT behind PA prison walls, prisonradio.org, the BOOKS THROUGH BARS project, the AMISTAD & ABOLITIONIST LAW CENTERS, respectively, the ONE-HOOD UNITED movement, and the many FAMILY &

FRIENDS and the consciously concerned in general, including Activist-Attorney Bret Grote, who is quickly becoming our Movement's (and our generation's) William Kuntzler; Patricia "Momma Pat" Vickers, Shandra Delaney, Karen Lee, Theresa Shoatz, Karen Ali, Sandra "Nehanda" Hill, Darrell "Shark" Phinizee, Richard "Tut" Carter, Atiba Kwesi, Bro. Yusef, Luqman Allah and countless others.

But I would be remiss if I failed to acknowledge the inspiration, creativity and selfless spirit of my communal niece Paris Morgan Schell, a 12 year-old Freedom Fighter, who drew a picture of the sun and mailed it to me when I was in the 'hole', thinking I had been placed into a literal hole (in the ground) and was unable to see the sun :-)

It is for her future and the future of her generation that I stand today against state-imposed tyranny. The tyranny that's being passed off as "LAW & ORDER". And it is - in a more broader sense - you, The People, who have helped me maintain my humanity while enduring this inhumane state of existence. And for that, I thank you!

IN SOLIDARITY,
Asafo Unchained!

iv

I CAN'T BREATHE ⊕

I CAN'T BREATHE

within the solitary confinement
of police-state policies
eleven times - ignored cries
until an "illegal" chokehold
silenced me

I CAN'T BREATHE

asphyxiated by mass incarceration
fixated on eradicating access
to public education

I CAN'T BREATHE

beneath the weight
of state-sanctioned hatred
unleashed unabated
onto a forsaken generation

I CAN'T BREATHE

pepper sprayed & handcuffed
hands up In Ferguson
no weapon displayed - not enough
man down - a murdered son

I CAN'T BREATHE

choking on the smoke & mirrors
of corporate-controlled
tell-lie-vision
promoting notions of hope & fairness
in co-opted grand jury decisions

I CAN'T BREATHE

muzzled, incommunicado
wondering what Obama would say
about prison hunger strikes
& struggles
from Cali to ADX Colorado
and Guantanamo Bay

I CAN'T BREATHE

swallowed into the jaws
of extra-judicial madness
& waterboard tortures
shrouded under laws enacted
to suppress the much less fortunate

I CAN'T BREATHE

en/trapped
within the narrow margins
of democracy's hypocrisies
and 'probable-cause' liabilities
pushed back
into the shadows of "harmless"
'color-blind' fallacies
& plausible deniabilities

I CAN'T BREATHE

12 years a child
shot down by guile
a toy gun = a lost life
covered by hatred & lies
foisted tongues & racial profiles

I CAN'T BREATHE

because my dark hue
causes a re/public nuisance
arousing the ire of the agents
of empire
and their colorful stooges
publicly lynched until i expire
by 'blue' palms fashioned like nooses
for the 'high' crimes
of bartering black-market loosies

I CAN'T BREATHE

In Amerikkka!

Asafo Unchained

SLAVERY: HERE & NOW

CONTRARY TO POPULAR BELIEF that the EMANCIPATION PROCLAMATION of 1863 actually ended slavery for Afrikans here in North America, it has not! And although it has taken on more subtle variations to suit the changing times & trends, an honest examination of the enduring powerless lot of Afrikan peoples would certainly lend credence to the familiar maxim: 'The More Things Change The More They Remain The Same.' Sure, the chains were removed from the hands & feet of captured Afrikans but they were alternately placed on their minds, thus choreographing their prescribed behavior within the broader American society. However, when it comes to the mass incarceration of Afrikan men, women & children within what has become widely referred to as, the Prison Industrial Complex, we see the continuum of chattel slavery; concealed of course, behind the rubric of "CRIME & PUNISHMENT". The term 'CRIMINAL' itself is a loaded handle, wielded by white power-holders to perpetuate the imprisonment (enslavement) of Afrikans, enshrined within its more ubiquitous phrase: "LAW & ORDER". A phrase interpreted by many of us Afrikans, in the context of its dual functioning, as it adversely effects us versus European-Americans, to mean our systemic entrapment.

And given what Earl Ofari Hutchenson so fittingly termed, "The Assassination Of The Black Male Image", by the biased corporate-owned media machine; the spurious social science and the manipulated religious interpretations which painted God in the image of a European while deeming Afrikans cursed, and thus worthy of an eternal status of inferiority, gives us an historical foundation for the ways & means by which the politics of "race" are being played out in the now-times; Especially as it pertains to the criminalization of Afrikans.

In her eye-opening treatise: "THE NEW JIM CROW", Michelle Alexander very cogently explains how an entire nation of captured

1

Afrikans can be wantonly, maliciously and deliberately targeted for mass incarceration and subsequently relegated to a permanent undercaste status here in the "Land Of The Free ..." by laws, statutes & policies that appear race-neutral (on their face) while being enforced in lieu of a sinister political agenda that ultimately serves the aims & objectives of this ivory-coated empire called America, at the expense of those people the white oppressors have always considered to be, in the words of warrior-scholar Marimba Ani, "The Cultural Other."

In this vein, Alexander's study succeeds in peeling back the veil of "color-blindness", revealing with empirical data (the bulk of which was gleaned from the state's own archives), not only the racist & biased ways in which the laws are still being applied to the "Cultural Other", but how the state's economy, power dynamics & status quo, much like the Jim Crow era of old, is dependent upon its NEW version which we're faced with today; so much so, that, it cannot turn itself around. It therefore reinvents itself in different guises in an attempt to evade scrutiny while shrouding itself in "color-blind" rhetoric which itself is monopolized (i.e., framed, controlled & contextualized) by the state, in terms of when and how racial matters should be presented, discussed or handled in the society at large, but especially so within the political/Law & Order realm.

But once we decode the Greco-Latin "legal" jargon and remove the esoteric mask as to how it protects white rule while, conversely, subjugating Afrikan peoples, it reveals the naked face of its hypocrisy. Take, for example, the term "EMANCIPATE", which is said to mean 'To Set Free'. However, when traced back to its origins, we learn that it is a term taken from old Roman legalese, and REALLY means: Transfer Of Ownership. So Afrikan captives were never truly "Set Free". We were merely transferred from private property status to state-owned property, which later became known as "Assumable Jurisdiction".

Hell, the "Emancipator" himself (Abraham Lincoln), during his

2

debates with political opponent Stephen Douglas, declared: "There must be an inferior and a superior; I as much as any man, am in favor of Superior being assigned to the white race." So when we look at the systematic condemnation, demonization and subsequent criminalization of Afrikans through the prism of the double-edged 13th Amendment to the United States constitution, which reads:

> "Neither slavery nor involuntary servitude, except as a punishment for crime whereof the party shall have been duly convicted, shall exist within the United States, or any place subject to their jurisdiction."

It brings into clearer focus the rise & proliferation of today's new slave plantations euphemistically called "Correctional Facilities." In fact, it is no empty coincidence that just after the close of the Civil War (April 1865) Afrikans in America's prisons immediately went from zero to over 30%. Afrikan prisoners were then subject to the brutal convict-lease system where forced free prison labor was leased out to plantation-owners and other industrial barons, filling the coffers of prison wardens and the states' respective treasuries; an arrangement described in David M. Oshinsky's titled book, as "WORSE THAN SLAVERY." Fast-forward to the now-times and - as we can see - the three fastest growing industries are: the Military Industrial Complex, the Prison Industrial Complex and the Surveillance Industrial Complex, all working in concert to more efficiently maintain the colonization, surveillance and imprisonment (enslavement) of the ghettos and their Afrikan denizens (not excluding poor whites).

Each state's court system serves as the new slave owners, a system driven by coded policies; with elected politicians performing in the capacity of modern-day slave traders, and the police apparatus acting as today's slave hunters/catchers. America's jails & prisons are of course the new slave plantations, where forced cheap prison labor is in full force. Prison industrial sweatshops throughout the United States produce everything, from car parts to pillowcases (and much in between), which are matriculated into the wider consumer market flow, at great profits.

Prisoners are also sacrificed at the alter of exploitation, at the hands of rapacious private sector profiteers, e.g., Telephone companies, transportation services, Prison commissary vendors, Money order/wire-transfer firms, Cable companies, etc., etc., etc., with handsome kickbacks paid to the prisonocracy.

SLAVES NEVER HELD WEALTH IN COMMON WITH MASTERS

THE COMMONWEALTH OF PENNSYLVANIA, a state which holds some 50,000 (fifty-thousand) men, women and children (juveniles) behind the walls and fences of its new-age plantations,have a unique history. Being one of the original 13 colonies, it is steeped in the rich tradition of chattel slavery, a tradition that is alive and thriving as we speak. The very emblem, on the commonwealth flag, which flies over every municipal building (and every single prison & jail) in the state of Pennsylvania, and stamped atop all official state charters, is an old and persistent symbol of slavery.

It was originally used in the south, to identify "legitimate" auction blocks where European-American males sold and traded captured Afrikan men, women & children. It also represented a Bill Of Sales. If you look closely, between the two raised horses you will see a slaveship, which represents the trafficking in human cargo. Just beneath the slaveship is a farm hoe, which signifies the labor of the

4

enslaved on the many plantations, as the backbone of the state's economy. The three bales of Cotton, Wheat &, Tobacco represent the principle crops that enriched the slave master's society. The eagle (or vulture) that sits at the very top represents insatiable greed.

These emblems (Coat of Arms) are still used today on all uniforms and documents that continues to perpetuate this modern form of slavery. The Pennsylvania Department Of Corrections (PA D.O.C.), the courts, D.A.'s, lawyers, Parole & Probation, et al. , all use this symbol to signify that they are continuing the original plantation business; only in a slightly different and more "accepted" form.

****

IT IS BENEATH THE PALL of the aforementioned facts, and a gross lack of prior knowledge of said politics of imprisonment (new enslavement) that I find myself condemned to die a Death By Incarceration here in one of Pennsylvania's most wretched slave camps.

My journey into this particular circle of hell began, not unlike many other captured Afrikans who find themselves similarly situated, as a youngster growing up in the hood, struggling to grapple with the dregs of poverty and social isolation. Little did I know my life's course was pretty much charted. Born to parents Rita Williams and Robert Allen, in the fall of '69, a period when social upheaval was in the air and liberation movements around the world were under the gun (literally) by neo-colonial forces hell-bent on maintaining a white world order, my parents had high hopes for their baby boy despite my beginnings being in a small apartment of a housing project in the "Black-Bottom" section of west Philadelphia.

The early 70's throughout the early 80's saw heroin wrack the black ghettos, in what many believed to be an integral part of the federal government's plot to snuff out any remnants of Black militancy after imprisoning, co-opting, assassinating and chasing into exile cadres of Black Liberation leaders. My parents were not exempt from the drug-use of the times.

They would eventually part ways when I was just a small child. My mother, however, even while just barely keeping her head above water, would have another child, my sister Lonia, by another man, and some four years later, my brother John, by another. We were, like many others in our community, constantly in financial straits, and almost wholly dependent upon the welfare system, therefore living hand-to-mouth. However, even this tenuous sense of stability wouldn't last long, as my brother, sister and me would watch, helplessly, as our (single) mother descended into the abyss of alcoholism - an illness that neither of us could fully comprehend at the time - nor were we (psychologically) prepared for the devastation it would eventually have on all our young lives.

As her situation worsened, and me being the oldest, I could discern the diminishing parental guidance/authority, so I began to hooky from school until I ceased attending altogether. I became an elementary school dropout. And the streets was ready to receive me with open arms. An early memory of mines - and perhaps - in retrospect, an harbinger of the urban survival skills I would later rely on to navigate the treacherous terrain of street-life, was when I expropriated a loaf of bread and some lunchmeat from a local supermarket, to feed my younger siblings. I was maybe 13 years-old. When it became apparent that our mother could no longer care for us we were cast to the wind (so to speak). My brother went with his father, my sister with our maternal grandmother, and me, well, I floated between the streets, my aunt Sandy's spot, my paternal grandmother's place (both in the Mill Creek housing projects) and eventually becoming a regular resident of the state's many juvenile facilities which, looking back now, was a mere dress-rehearsal for a more seamless transition into the adult prison (plantation) system. It was within the juvenile prison system where I witnessed (and experienced) open racism and brutality at the hands of facility administrators and the day-to-day overseers, all within the broader

6

white supremacist ideal - an ideal I simply could not comprehend at the time that is, until I listened to some vintage speeches by Malcolm X on cassette tapes smuggled in by a concerned Afrikan elder (staff member), where Malcolm gives context to Blacks' plight here in America.

And while Malcolm's words resonated within my very ethos, and even answered some of the pressing questions of the moment, there was still something missing; and although I couldn't quite put my finger on it, the seed was planted. Yeah, Malcolm's words would open up my eyes, enabling me to see things a little differently. But I was still faced with the immediate reality of being dispossessed from the first group of people I knew in the world - my family.

I pushed the pain (and the shame) of my displacement deep down into my soul, figuring it would just go away. But it didn't. Instead, it would, on a subconscious level, have the greatest influence on my behavior, in terms of how I interacted within the society, but especially so with my peers who - likewise - were experiencing their own variations of the same brand of destitution.

We roamed the Black colony like virtual nomads, in search of a sense of belonging. And with little or no parental guidance, or a constructive Rites Of Passage system to bring forth and mold our God-given potentials, we clung to the streets. We boosted food, clothes & funds to sustain ourselves; and smoked weed, popped pills and sipped codeine-laced cough syrup to numb the pain, and to escape a reality that our (induced) fear and (acquired) ignorance precluded us from confronting head-on.

We vied for street-cred and "respect" within our respective hoods by posturing like heartless thugs and engaging in fist-fights and the occasional gun play, with the convoluted rationale being: The More Heartless The Individual The More Respected. A fratricidal conditioning that would make behavioral psychologist B.F. Skinner look like a prophet. Still, Malcolm's words were taking root.

THE MID 80's brought with it an extinction-level event that would smite the Black ghettos like a curse, ravaging its moral fiber. It came like a thief in the night and stole the very souls of whole communities, both user & dealer alike; A pestilence of biblical proportions, with its ramifications still being felt in the present (some 30 years later). Its name is Crack-cocaine. From the jump, it shifted priorities, values and the remaining vestiges of communal principles & practices, to that of a callous disregard for one's fellow-man, hyperindividualism, and a covetous greed accompanied by extreme violence, thus despair.

At just 14 years-old, this was an overload on my sensibilities. That I was in gun battles with my own peers, sustaining bullet wounds on several occasions before my 20th birthday, is a testament to the avarice-sphere (environment of greed) that the hood had become. It was every man for himself!

When it was finally exposed by San Jose Mercury news investigative journalist Gary Webb, that the CIA was behind the Crack epidemic that devastated the entire Black colony, to finance a (dirty little secret) war against other dark-skinned peoples in the Central American country of Nicaragua, it did not come as a big surprise, as even in my ignorance - and yet unable to discern its full scope - I had enough sense to know that it didn't just appear out of thin air, and, by some (bad) luck of the draw, land in the urban centers of America. Besides, Malcolm's words were sprouting within my mind, rousing me from my (mental) slumber.

At age 15, while serving yet another juvenile stint, I would meet a woman who would have a huge impact on my life, who helped restore my conscience. She nurtured me like a mother would a son, and seemed to understand me without inquiry; she was able to cut through the static that clouded my reasoning, and direct my focus toward higher ideals. Her role, over the years, would expand to include counselor, confidant & comrade. Her name is Sandra "Nehanda" Hill. An often repeated yet simple refrain of hers, which would connect me to Malcolm's words in a more purposeful way, was: "Your life has a purpose, don't waste it." The compassionate words of this soft-spoken woman combined with the fiery oratory of Malcolm X echoed in my spirit and began to move me. But my greatest struggle would be just up ahead.

****

BY THE AGE OF 17, and tired of being a part of the "problem", I decided it was time for a change; so I enrolled into the Nation Of Islam and began studying the life-saving teachings of its founder Msssenger Elijah Muhammad. My inherited slave surname was summarily replaced by an X until I was later re-named Asafo Chuma Asafo. Within the movement's ranking structure I was appointed to the position of Captain and then Field-General, with the responsibility of recruiting, teaching & training other wayward inner-city youth, in the importance of Unity, their History, Culture and heritage.

Young Asafo

However, by 19, I was back in the clutches of "the system". This time for the killing of a local drug dealer. At my trial I was precluded from defending myself and was given a court-appointed attorney (officer of the court) whose defense (or lack thereof) resulted in a 2nd degree murder conviction, thus an (automatic) sentence of Life-Without-Parole. A sentence tantamount to death (by attrition). In this age of mass incarceration, it's not even necessary for us to elaborate on the biased tenets of America's judicial system, to get a grasp of its insatiable appetite for swallowing up its so-called "citizens" (over 2 million & counting) - with the overwhelming majority being Afrikan and other non-white peoples; not excluding poor whites.

In my criminal case, I never denied culpability; only to a lesser degree than what was found by the courts. Even the evidence of record reflects as much.

I was convicted by a jury in 1990, of second-degree murder (and robbery) which, in the state of Pennsylvania, carries a sentence of Life (or Death By Incarceration). An initial review of some of the most obvious facts prompted the court to immediately eliminate first-degree, as the court recognized from the outset that there was neither premeditation nor intent.

However, because I was charged and convicted of the robbery (a felony) which was tenuously buttressed as the "motive", it aggravated the murder charge. The law in the state of Pennsylvania says that: 'If A Murder Occurs During The Commission Of A Felony(Even If Murder Isn't The Initial Intent), It Constitutes Second-Degree, thus Life.'

Grossly overlooked was the fact that I never committed a robbery nor intended to. This much was originally attested to by the state's own witnesses. Yet I was still convicted of the fabled robbery charge. Amidst the smoke-screen of a case presented by the state - the truth became the first casualty.

THE TRUTH IS: The entire misadventure that left one Afrikan dead and another imprisoned evolved from a confrontation between us when I tried to get the decedent to leave the apartment of a former girlfriend (and her two small children) which the decedent (and company) had converted into a crack cocaine manufacturing & packaging spot.

Ironically, it was the state's threats to take away her children (for allowing their home to be used as a drug den) that compelled her to allow the truth to be covered up and essentially acquiesce to the concocted "robbery" narrative; also to evade prosecution for such activity; thereby consigning me to a Life of imprisonment. Because without "robbery" as a motive this entire unfortunate ordeal would have amounted to a third-degree (or less), which would have rendered me eligible for parole some 15 years ago, or completely maxed-out some 5 years ago. Needless to say, I am still experiencing the ongoing devastation of such an unjust conviction and subsequent sentence of Death By Incarceration; a devastation that was equal parts proportionate to my initial naivete and ignorance of the law or, better yet, the politics of how the "law" is applied to Afrikans in this racist society.

Moreover, being fleeced out of thousands of hard earned dollars by what proved to be shyster attorneys hired to appeal my reversible issues to the state's high courts, only to be repeatedly shot down by the courts and then summarily discarded by said lawyers, I began to see things for what they really are; not only for myself, but for all those who are similarly situated.

The entire judicial system (including the appeals process) has nothing to do with "justice" or any concept of 'Right' & 'Wrong' - as rhetorically proffered by the state - it's all politics, politics, politics: The Politics of Race, The Politics of Imprisonment (Enslavement) and The Politics of power.

****

CONSIDER THESE 6 POINTS

• At just 19 years-old at the time of my arrest, and according to the Pennsylvania Constitution, I was a juvenile. See Constitution of The Commonwealth of Pennsylvania Article 5 § Section 16 (q) (ii): 'Juvenile Matters', where the article is clear and unambiguous as it makes the distinction between two classes of juveniles and set forth the legal definitions and age ranges of two classes of juveniles as

11

such: "Children as a person under 18 years of age and Minors as 18 to 21 years of age."

Moreover, in the wake of the 2012 Miller & 2016 Montgomery rulings, respectively, where, in the former, the United States Supreme Court ruled that Life-Without-Parole for juveniles is a violation of the 8th Amendment and thus unconstitutional; with the latter (2016) Montgomery ruling making the (2012) Miller ruling retroactive, rendering hundreds of Pennsylvania's Juvenile Lifers, who have been languishing in the state's prisons, eligible for parole.

But the myopic views of many legal pundits seems to be stalled at an "age" impasse, rigidly sticking to the "under 18" portion of the rulings, and ignoring the mention of "minors" in the United States Supreme Court's 50 page opinion, and, interestingly dismissing out-of-hand the compelling Brief by the American Psychological Association, American Psychiatric Association and the National Association Of Social Workers whose collective study and findings the U.S. Supreme Court relied upon to reach its decision.

In their Brief, filed along with the Miller appeal, many of the study group members found that the developmental maturity of juveniles goes well into the mid-twenties. Furthermore, the notion that the individual states are strictly bound by the "under 18" portion of the U.S. Supreme Court's language - and stripped of their (state) power to apply their own respective constitutions to the plight of juveniles - has been effectively debunked by the case of Chicago native Antonio House who, at age 19, was convicted of a double-homicide and sentenced to Life-Without-Parole, which was subsequently overturned, remanded for re-sentencing, citing the (Illinois) state's constitution (See PEOPLE V. HOUSE 2015, IL APP 1st 110580).

In another twist of irony, the National Rifle Association (NRA), on behalf of several of its youth members, brought a federal civil action in a Texas District Court against the Bureau of Alcohol, Tobacco & Firearms (ATF), for precluding the youths from purchasing handguns from federally licensed gun dealers based on their age ranges, which were between 18 & 20; the court ruled in favor of the defendants (ATF), agreeing that, since neither of the plaintiffs were yet 21 , they weren't (mentally) mature enough to possess handguns (a ruling affirmed by the U.S. Court of Appeals for the 5th Circuit). See: NRA V. ATF, 700 F. 3d 185 (5th Cir. 2012).

The contradictions are clear, and shows how the laws are applied like a double-edged blade, slicing whichever way the law makers deem necessary, to suit their political aims - often leaving the poor in general but Afrikans in particular - with the shortest slice of "Justice".

Maybe if I was a rich white kid from suburban texas (Ethan Couch) and admittedly guilty of multiple counts of murder, I could have gotten off with a slap on the wrist, by using the invented "AFFLUENZA" defense, avoiding jail time altogether. Instead, my reality was/is the complete opposite: POOR, AFRIKAN (BLACK) and FROM THE GHETTO. I guess you could say I suffer from an acute case of 'BROKE-FOLKS-SCLEROSIS'.

* Recently, several witnesses who testified against me in my original trial have come forth to clear the record about the fabled "robbery" charge, emphasizing that it never occurred. One witness was himself a juvenile (17 years-old) when he was questioned without a parent or guardian, admitted that he simply went along with the robbery offense, at the insistence of Assistant district attorney William Boland.

Another witness who would not go along with the robbery story was blocked from testifying altogether, which was kept secret until recently.

And yet another was given a deal, in an unrelated case, for his false testimony, which was also kept secret, even when questioned about it in open court. The conviction for the spurious robbery charge is the underlying element holding this unjust Life sentence over me. Without it, this ominous Death By Incarceration or Life

13

sentence would have to be rescinded and a lesser sentence issued. WHERE IS THE JUSTICE?

* Another significant element that just came to light is that -to aid me after filing a PCRA petition pro se - the Pennsylvania Superior court knowingly & deliberately appointed me a defective attorney (James S. Bruno) back In 1999 who, by his own admission before a disciplinary board, was experiencing serious psychological issues dating back to the 80's, which is a matter of record. Mr. Bruno's flagrant derelict of duty and irresponsibility to his imprisoned clients came to a head when a throng of his clients complained to the Disciplinary Board about his wanton negligence, culminating in Bruno having his Bar license suspended for 2 years. In my case, Mr. Bruno filed a Finley-Letter to shirk his appointment duties to my case, by citing inaccurate information to support his claim that my PCRA petition lacked merit. SEE: padisciplinaryboard.org and Disciplinary counsel v. James S. Bruno 1910 Docket No.3 (180 DB 2011). Again, WHERE IS THE JUSTICE?

* In 2015 a Philadelphia woman (Rochelle Dukes) filed a $20 million lawsuit against former, supervising judge of the Philadelphia common pleas court trial division, William J. Manfredi, for conspiring with the prothonotary Joseph Evers, to purposefully sabotage a prior (2011) civil action against Manfredi's friend and fellow judge Jacquilne Allen, by wantonly blocking plaintiff Rochelle Dukes' motion to proceed in Forma Pauperis; with the prothonotary Joseph Evers concealing the docket entry in another file. Manfredi

Manfredi also maliciously dismissed as frivolous an earlier (2009) lawsuit filed by Ms. Dukes against the Walker Memorial training Center. SEE: Case ID #120501133.

This seems to be a pattern of former judge Manfredi's; a pattern that harkens back to my 1990 trial. Yeah, the "honorable" judge Manfredi presided over the homicide trial of this writer, and ultimately condemned me to die a Death By Incarceration (Life-

14

Without-Parole) - even lecturing me during the sentencing phase, that: 'Given my juvenile history, lack of formal schooling, unstable home life, etc., the sentence he was poised to impose seemed an inevitable conclusion to my life.' Of more relevance here though, was his stubborn refusal to properly instruct the jury - during the deliberation phase of the trial and upon jury request, on the definitions of the lesser charges of Third-Degree and Manslaughter, respectively; instead urging the jury members to concentrate on second-Degree, exclusively.

This was a clear case of Abuse Of Authority and Official Oppression. Yet this 'Abuse' was dismissed as 'harmless' by his colleagues/compatriots in the state's higher courts. After all, Superior & Supreme court jurists are all a part of the same (political) fraternity. Consistent with the politics of Black inferiority, their wealth and political careers are built on the backs of the imprisoned (enslaved). Sure, they grant an appeal every so often, to maintain the appearance that "The System" works, to 'keep hope alive' in the hearts & minds of destitute prison dwellers.

But the currency is in the convictions; both literal & political So the unethical - even criminal - practices of judges, at every level of the lopsided "Criminal Justice System" to maintain the 'conviction' quota, has become routine; so much so that It has even become difficult to distinguish magistrates from miscreants further highlighting the sharpening contradictions of race-based "Law & Order".

* While there are thousands of us captured Pennsylvania prisoners fighting an already (steep) uphill battle to regain our physical liberation from within the grip of the relentless beast that is the state's prison system, especially from beneath the omen of the well-honed stigma of being eternally criminalized, and even from within the shadow of Hillary Clinton's "Super Predator" designation which, by the way, was in support of her husband's 1994 Crime Bill. which not only contributed greatly to the exponential growth of prison

construction all around the country, to accommodate the mass incarceration of Afrikans (Blacks), Latinos and even poor whites, but it adversely effected the appeals process. For example, while there is no 'Statute-Of-Limitations' on murder, one convicted of same has only one year to correct any errors the courts may have made during the trial. It even restricted the scope of the Habeas Corpus process.

So just imagine the slap-in-the-face level of disgust of many of us prisoners trapped here In Pennsylvania's prisons, to witness the outright crimes and immoral acts of the very custodians of the state's jurisprudence either covered up or down-played - as in the "porn-gate" scandal of Philadelphia's Assistant District Attorneys Frank Fina and Marc Constanza, where they both use porn imagery to illustrate their lewd commentary which belittles and denigrates women in the workplace; while their boss Philadelphia District Attorney Seth Williams defended their behavior.

Then there's the racist rhetoric & crass sexual "humor" discovered in the emails of disgraced Pennsylvania Supreme Court Justice Michael Eakins. And the 234 pornographic emails, even of little children, sent and received by Pennsylvania Supreme Court Justice Seamus McCaffery. The list is actually too extensive to point out every single instance here; but I think the public gets the point. A simple Google search of those mentioned, or a brief visit to the site - judicialmisfits.com and other related links will most certainly offer the concerned public a view into just how deep the (hypocritical) rabbit-hole goes!

* Then there is the looming question of the very "legality" of the "Life Sentence" itself in the state of Pennsylvania; a question that is growing increasingly unavoidable, demanding of an answer that is commensurate with what is actually outlined in the state's "laws", as opposed to what has become "common practice". And being held captive for nearly three decades under the shady pretext of an ambiguous 2nd degree murder conviction, it bears significance that

16

we question the most glaring contradictions in both the 'conviction' and the state-imposed 'Life Sentence'.

To begin with, the whole stage - for this entire judicial fiasco - was set with the "INDICTMENT", which never specified (as required by law) a particular charge or degree of murder; instead using the customary "open charge" of murder under the 18 Pa. C.S. § 2501 Criminal Homicide only to later settle on 18 Pa. C.S. § 1102 (b) second-degree murder, which was a blatant violation of my Due Process. I mean, how could I possibly prepare a defense 'against that which was not made clear to begin with? This is to say, if 2nd degree was the criminal charge then the 'Bill Of Indictment" should have read: 18 Pa. C.S. § 2502 (b), Murder of The Second-Degree The right to a formal notice of the specific charges is guaranteed by the Sixth Amendment of the Federal Constitution and by Article 1, Section 9 of the Pennsylvania Constitution. So arbitrary and haphazard was the handling of the charges that my trial was originally staged as a 'Capital' (death penalty) qualified case, with the impaneled jury advised of such, and then later advised, after hearing the testimony of the first witness, that, it was not a 'Capital' case, and that the jury should just disregard such prior advice. A GOD-DAMNED SHAME!

THE SCALES OF HYPOCRISY

****

Furthermore, since no 'Sentencing Order' was ever issued - in accordance with 42 Pa. C.S. § 9764 (a) (8) - my confinement is essentially unlawful. The "Judgment Of Sentence" document is one of the single most significant documents issued from the sentencing judge because it is the only document that officially (lawfully) verifies that a defendant has actually been convicted of a criminal offense; That the defendant has been sentenced by a court of law; That there is a lawful court order that allows the PA Department of Corrections

17

to receive the prisoner into its custody as mandated by <u>37 Pa. Code 91.3</u>.

Moreover, the Pennsylvania, Rules of Appellate Procedure, at chapter 3 in particular, outlines the imperative of "Orders From Which Appeals May Be Taken". This is to say, quite plainly, that, ALL appeals: DIRECT; PCRA; STATE or FEDERAL HABEAS CORPUS, etc. Must First Have Some Type Of Order For The Appellant To Appeal From.

After all, how could one possibly (lawfully) appeal that which doesn't (lawfully) exist? Again,WHERE IS THE JUSTICE?

For a more, fuller and detailed breakdown of the full scope of this matter please visit PAsentencing.com or write to: P.O. Box 98157 Pittsburgh, PA 15227 or call @412.253-5593

SLAVERY BY THE NUMBERS

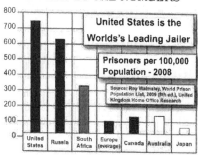

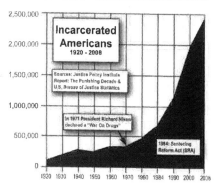

FREEDOM FIGHTERS

Rusell Shoatz Jr.

Shandra Delaney

Kianga & Sandra

A young Asafo

Patricia "Momma Pat" Vickers

FIGHT FOR LIFERS

Paris M. Schell

19

Momma Pat, Theresa, Sandra & Bret Grote

Sandra "Nehanda" Hill & Theresa

Bro. Luqman

Shark & Asafo

AN ELDER MILITARY VETERAN Jaffar Saidi once told me that when a soldier is conscripted to engage in a war, especially one where the shedding of blood on both sides is witnessed and experienced up close & personal, it forces that soldier to look beyond the 'official' rationale for the conflict in search of the REAL (political) objective that's being promoted. Well, being a long-held captive member of the incarcerated class, shuttled between many of Pennsylvania's most repressive prisons and subjected to its torturous solitary confinement chambers has, likewise, prompted me to question the REAL motives of the "legal" system and to ultimately connect the dots to the lopsided social construct itself.

For many years, "criminality", social deviance and what have you, had been projected and therefore regarded by the public at large, as forms of sociopathic behavior that had no connection to the mainstream social order. That is, until the politics of imprisonment as a leading tentacle of the capitalist empire state (America) was exposed as a method to manage and control its Afrikan and other non-white 'undesirables' as well as a tool of socio-political repression, and for neo-enslavement; even exposing the foisted  'bell-Curve' theory as fraudulent racist propaganda which depicts us Afrikans as having "A Natural-born Propensity Toward Crime", to justify our criminalization and subsequent mass imprisonment (enslavement).

Conversely, in traditional Afrikan societies, for instance, if a person stole something the society didn't necessarily deem that person the "lone" perpetrator per se, as the entire society would come under scrutiny. For it reasoned that, if one was compelled to steal within a society where the tenets of the social order are grounded in communal sharing, then what has the society done, in terms of the distribution of the resources (or neglect of same) to cause one to steal (in the first place).

21

America, however, is a society that doesn't subscribe to such logic. For it is a society predicated on - at its very foundation - "Slaves & Masters", "Bosses & Workers", "The Privileged & The Poor", "The Haves & The Have-nots" which, as it necessitates, are interchangeable with "Cops & Robbers", "Good-guys & Bad-guys" and what not, whereby it becomes perfectly normal to accept a group (or class) of people having complete power over the very access to such human necessities as Education, Medical care, Food, Clothing, Shelter, and every other human resource, while other (racial) groups (or classes) doesn't (within the same society). These are the class & racial contradictions that forms the axis upon which American-style "LAW & ORDER" revolves, with the powerless portrayed as socially inept, thus "naturally" precluded from higher class ideals;, thereby, inherently prone to crime or social deviance in general; a proclivity endemic to that class or racial group alone, void of any congenital nexus to its avaricious progenitor. Such is the hypocrisy. And to this dense line of reasoning, an 18th century poet once quipped that: "The law will punish a man or woman who steals the goose from the hillside, but let's the greater robber loose who steals the hillside from the goose."

****

LEGAL SLAVERY DECODED

"I think God intended the niggers to be slaves. Now since man has deranged God's plan, I think the best we can do is keep 'em near to a state of bondage as possible. ... My theory is, feed 'em well, clothe 'em well, and then, if they don't work ... whip 'em well."

- A YAZOO DELTA PLANTER, 1866 - FROM DAVID M. OSHINSKY'S BOOK: "WORSE THAN SLAVERY" p.11

22

The word SLAVE is typically defined as a condition where one is completely under the power of another. Where one has no freedom of action; whose person and services are wholly under the control of a master, and subject to forced servitude. Can be sold or bought or otherwise disposed of at the whim of a master, without being able to do anything of his or her own free will.

This definition is pretty much universal, as many different ethnic groups, even individuals, throughout history - and throughout the world - have experienced their respective versions and variations of what is commonly offered as a general description of what a slave or slavery is. In fact, the word SLAVE is said to have its origins in the word SLAV for the mass subjugation of the Slavic peoples in central Europe in the middle ages, by other Europeans of course. However, Afrikan peoples are the only people in the history of the world whose enslavement, by Europeans, beginning in the 15th century, carry the unique distinction of being permanent. The essential objective of slavery, after all, is the

TORTURED FREEDOM-FIGHTER

dominion of one person or group of people over another person or group of people, for exploitative purposes. The systematic infliction of terror & violence upon the bodies & minds of the subject person or group is essential to compliance along with a controlled environment, labor objectives, etc., even in the short term.

But when a people are forcibly taken from their homeland, and have their entire culture systematically ripped from them, i.e., languages, names, customs, spiritual systems, communatarian principles & practices and, most of all, their will to resist, and made the de facto property of another (from private to state-owned), as prominently indicated by the slave-names that are still being carried by Afrikans in America today; even the "Christian" (or European) names in general, are the markings of permanence. Actually, to carry the names, titles, designations, brands, etc., that were forced on us at the very inception of our enslavement, and carried from generation to generation into the present, is fundamental to one's acceptance of and identification with oneself as being State-Property here & now in this 21st century.

Names, Titles, Designations and the like, are often taken to be insignificant or benign, especially by the culturally impaired and the uninformed.

Conversely, it is within one's identity, one's TRUE nationality, that true freedom is pursued. So it logically follows that one's bondage (in the permanent sense), exists in the opposite. Nigger/Negro, Black, Colored, African-American and other hollow handles given to us by European enslavers keep us strategically separated from our true national identity and eternally bound to them as property. Furthermore, there is no such national territory called Negro or Black or Colored or what have you. In fact, they are purely American inventions and are pretty much confined within her borders.

This bears great significance within the context of American Jurisprudence. Afrikans simply cannot effectively approach their liberation from the posture of slaves (property) and expect their 'Rights' to be respected. An historical example of this can be found in the 1857 Dred Scott decision which stated: "The negro has no rights that the true citizen (white man) are bound to respect." In Dred Scott-V.-Sanford the United States Supreme Court essentially ruled that Dred Scott (as a slave) was not a "citizen"; but was in fact property and had no 'rights' or 'privileges', therefore must remain enslaved. Scott's argument for his freedom was made from the tenuous position of 'A negro' (property), and not from the more viable position of a 'national sovereign' (a true flesh & blood Afrikan).

24

And since he failed to do so, his argument was - in the 'legal' context equal to that of a horse or a cow seeking 'legal' freedom from its owner. Absurd, right?

The reality is, Afrikans here in America are not considered "citizens"; only those of Euro-American nationality. America is Europe's daughter. So, Afrikans caught up in a legal system that is tailored exclusively to fit the objectives of Euro-American Rule & Dominance (white supremacy), while maintaining the designated role of 'property', i.e., Black, Negro, Colored and what not, will remain enslaved. This applies to both the imprisoned and those in the so-called "free society" alike. How else could we be more than a century & a half removed from the Dred Scott Supreme Court decision and still begging  white America to acknowledge something they never will, that: "Black Lives Matter"? "Blacks" (as property) aren't seen as human just as Black/Negro wasn't seen as a "citizen" in the 1857 Scott instance. This is why Afrikans can be gunned down by white cops in the urban centers of America; even lynched in police custody or choked out on a public sidewalk by white police officers and their colorful clones, with impunity; And furthermore make up the majority demographic of America's prison/plantation population, while being the minority nationality in white America. Have we forgotten the "3/5ths of a human" tag placed on us Afrikans by Euro-American lawmakers? 5/5ths constituted a 'whole' person or human; which consists of 1.) The Physical (the flesh & blood self), 2.) The Mental (the cognitive perceptive self), 3.) The Soul (power of thought, internal discernment, etc.), 4.) The Spirit (the eternal connection to the Creator) and 5.) Identity (ancestral lineage, name, nationality).

Numbers 4 & 5 are not recognized in Afrikans by the white slave-holders, thus deeming Afrikans 3/5ths of a human. The Euro-American 'logic' was/is that, any man bereft of his divine connection to his Creator and without his TRUE identity/nationality is essentially incomplete! This great American myth is woven into the very fabric of the American 'legal' system and, moreover, within the practical culture or credo of Euro-American thought & behavior toward Afrikan and other non-white peoples within the society at large.

So the concepts: "All men are created equal" and that the U.S. Constitution was written "By THE PEOPLE and For THE PEOPLE" did not have Afrikans in mind when they were conceived and written - and still don't. For us, during that time, it was literally illegal to read & write. And although the 14th Amendment to the constitution supposedly did away with the three-fifths-human edict, such an amendment proved to be merely nominal, as the treatment of Afrikans in America, especially in the "legal" framework, is still one of marginalization and dehumanization; never mind the euphemistic allusions to the contrary.

The enduring reality is that Afrikans are the eternal bête noire (of Euro-American making) and are not considered "persons" or "people". Much of the blunt and more explicit language has been codified to suit the changing times. So now 'criminal', 'super predator', ' incorrigible', 'convicted felon' and other coded pejoratives equals "Black" (Afrikan). This way, slavery(for one duly convicted of a crime) as ratified by the duplictous 13th Amendment, pursuant to its permanence, is given quarter in the rise and proliferation of the Prison Industrial Complex. The dye, as they say, has been cast, in terms of what Khalil Gibran Muhammad calls: "The Condemnation Of Blackness", which keeps the stage set for the continuum of slavery, in whatever form or guise Euro-America chooses to perpetuate it.

The phantom of "race", as a time-tested political current with Afrikans cast in the negative of course is the proverbial third-rail in the (American) society, which cannot be deactivated without arousing deeper cultural realities and perhaps causing the collapse of the 'superiority/inferiority' status quo; so the Euro-American power-holders simply ignore it, or deny that it even exists. Much like the way America refuses to acknowledge its many Political Prisoners. Because to admit that it has Political Prisoners held in its many gulags all around the country is to admit that they are in fact revolutionaries (and not criminals), and to admit or acknowledge revolutionaries is to acknowledge that the need for revolution exists, which says that something is wrong with the current state of affairs.

And we all know that the American government, in all its lopsidedness, could never openly admit such. The same is true of the often requested government apology to Afrikans in America for the enslavement of our honorable ancestors. The American government simply will not do it. How could it, when slavery is still in full effect?

This also gives context to the mounting cries for 'Reparations'. The approach for it has historically been from a posture of impotence. Just like Dred Scott a century & a half ago, who petitioned Euro-America's highest court for his freedom, from the posture of property (a negro) and was summarily dismissed, so goes Euro-Americans blatant disregard for Afrikans' Reparations plight. It is significant to point out here that, despite Dred Scott's failed attempt, there were actually scores of other similar cases from the period and earlier that were relatively successful; the most noted being the Amistad case of 1839 (made famous by the movie), where over 50 Afrikan captives aboard the Amistad vessel sailing from Cuba, overpowered their would be enslavers; a high seas revolt lead by West Afrikan Mende warrior Sengbe Pieh (re-named Joseph Cinque). After being imprisoned, the Afrikan captives mounted two fierce courtroom battles - one criminal (for mutiny, August 29, 1839) and the other civil (for their freedom, November 19, 1839) - ultimately prevailing in both. On January 13, 1840 the court ruled that the Afrikan captives were essentially kidnapped, in violation of international law, and ordered returned back to their homeland.

Unlike Scott, they fought both literally and "legally" from the position of Sui Juris (real flesh & blood persons/Afrikans) and in their TRUE nationality/names (not as property). This is a lesson for us Afrikans held captive here on America's new slave-ships (on dry land) in the now-times. Our collective national identity and declared sovereignty is fundamental to our true liberation. Several credible formations in the lineage of our liberation struggle here in America have constructed viable platforms to facilitate various methods of repatriation back into our culture and nationhood, most notably, the Nation Of Islam (NOI) and the Provisional Government of the Republic of New Afrika (PGRNA), respectively. The very word 'Nation' in <u>Nation</u> Of Islam is a recognition that Afrikans in America constitute a nation within a nation. The Honorable Elijah Muhammad, founder & patriarch of the Nation Of Islam, illustrated an ideal of Nationhood/Sovereignty under its flag of the Sun, Moon & Star; repudiating the slave masters surname (replacing it with an X); calling for a separate state/territory to establish an independent government for Black (Afrikan) people; also calling for the immediate release of Black people from America's prisons and its death houses.

Similarly, the Provisional Government of the Republic of New Afrika, a formation borne from the Black Government Conference convened by some 500 Black (Afrikan) nationalists, in Detroit, Michigan in the spring of '68, which called for the establishment of an independent New Afrikan government, consisting of 5 of the Southern Blackbelt states: Mississippi, Alabama, Georgia, South Carolina and Louisiana, under the Pan-Afrikan flag of RED, BLACK & GREEN.

I mention this segment of our rich history of struggle for freedom & self-determination, to direct our sights and energies beyond the debilitating condition of (psychological) plantation-paralysis so that we can move collectively toward our true freedom, using some of the applicable methods given to us by our most committed thinkers and most dedicated Movement/Nation builders both living and transitioned.

This writing is an appeal to THE PEOPLE. I have NO faith in "The System"; only THE PEOPLE'S ability to bend the system to its WILL. So It Is With You That I Cast My Lot!

In Solidarity,

Asafo - Unchained

OH, AND ANOTHER THING...

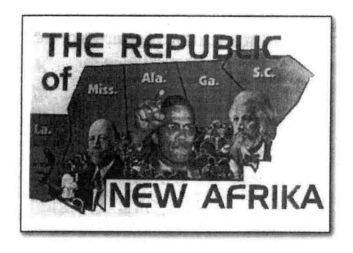

After the assassinations of Fred Hampton Sr., Dr. Martin Luther King Jr., George Jackson, Malcolm X and other Black Liberation leaders, the FBI, under the auspices of then director J. Edgar Hoover, issued a secret memo stating explicitly that it was/is the state's mission to thwart the rise of a "Black Messiah" or Black 'Warrior Class' from rising up out of the Black ghettos (including the prison system), that could electrify and mobilize the Black masses and ultimately usher in a full spectrum revolution. Well, we can see those orders have been carried out (and still are).

Over the past twenty or so years we have witnessed the gross 'Dumbing Down' of a large demographic of the society, where the politics that effects the very existence of The Masses, especially Afrikans, isn't even of concern, much less a topic of discussion; and even more less the impetus for organized resistance. Conversely, Sports & Entertainment, so-called "REALITY TV", the Life-styles (and gossip) of the 'Rich & Famous', Urban fiction (hood novels) and capitalist corporate canted news media, etc., have become the primary sources by which large segments of society are informed. Even Hip-Hop culture - which originally was a revolutionary street movement - have been hijacked and co-opted by capitalist corporate vultures and relegated to debased sexual imagery, gangsterism, the worship of materialism, images of make-believe power and an overall sense of 'Party & Bullshit'.

These have also become the diversions and main influences within the prison environment; keeping prisoners, much like their peers in the so-called 'free-world', in a perpetual state of ignorance, docility, individualism and disunity. So, rather than showing a logical interest in Revolutionary/Liberation praxis (theory & practice) - they have - iInstead contented themselves on 'Keeping Up With The Kardashians' and the like. SHAME!

We have also witnessed the widespread emergence of street-fraternities (so-called gangs), as well as the many religious factions, most of which have been completely denuded of their revolutionary zeal and now serve primarily as agents of disunity.

This has intensified significantly within the prisons. In fact, most of the street-fraternities within the prisons have been effectively co-opted by the prisons' respective internal intelligence/security departments. The same is true of many of the religious groups. While they all are listed as Security Threat Groups (S.T.G.'s), to justify any "official" aggressions against them, they are allowed (by the jailers) to act out their fratricidal (or inner-group) violence and ignorance, with impunity; so long as their activities are not geared toward forming alliances or progressive comradeships with rival gangs, or with religious groups, particularly with Islamic groups. Nevertheless, they all, for the most part, are manipulated and used by the jailers to perpetuate constant conflict, so the jailers can (collectively) control the entire environment one group at a time. Classic 'Divide & Conquer' (but on auto-pilot) and by remote control. Conversely, the CRIPS & BLOODS, for, example, who have returned to their Black Liberation roots: (Communal Revolution In Progress) and (Brotherly Love Over Oppression's Destruction), respectively, have come under "official" scrutiny for their willingness to work together; as well as for the likelihood of them politicizing their respective sets.

The jailers have already achieved a measure of success in keeping the 'moderate' or broke-back muslim factions separated from (and at odds with) the more militant elements, while, interestingly, keeping them all, to a significant degree, disengaged in Revolutionary/ Liberation praxis.

Rather, consigning all parties to mere religio-dogmatic rhetoric & rituals, devoid of the slightest modicum of resistance. The jailers have even 'hired' a class of obsequious muslim ministers and compromised (foreign) Imams & clerics to ensure the suppression of any revolutionary thought or activity. A modern crusade (if you will). Toward this end, in fact, recently, it has been revealed that

Homeland Security, at the behest of Zionist/Jewish interest groups, are actively providing funding to prison administrators to monitor their respective muslim populations, to pinpoint and weed out any so-called "radicalized" elements. Hence: The Institutionalization of Islam (of every stripe) is in full effect!

TO THE ASAFO YA UHURU CLAN (FAMILY) similarly situated here in state captivity: Knab A. Asafo, Kamau M. Asafo, Mtengenezi Asafo, Akode Asafo, Mandelek Asafo, Atiba D. Asafo and many other communal relatives, including our comrades & friends In the struggle: Shakaboona, Changa Asa Ramu, Saleem (Kreasy), Jabril A. Allah, Jerome "Hoag" Coffey, Man-Shareef, Ivan White, 17X, Arnet "Skip" Carter, Bryan "Mook" young, Saleem-Bendele, Ronald "Rock" Mason, Dave Henry, Bro. Tacoma, elder Joe-Joe "Old Man" Bowen, Rodney "Hoppo" Wells, elder Muhammad Kafl, elder Major Tillery, Lill Pica, Shaheed Kaos, Butchie Amir, Bro. Sabree, elder Sakin, Sugar Bear, elder Maroon, Kevin Qazim Johnson, Kaseem Grant, elder Harun Fox, Bro. Joshua Asadi, Lenny Basil, Craig Shadeed Haines, Bro. Jihad, Lil' Bub, Mumia Abu-Jamal, Suliaman Beyah, Bro. Uzo, Courtney "Juan" Boyd, elder Jaffar Saidi, Andre Shabaka, elder Ali, elder Omar Askia Ali, Malcolm Rowe, Hakim sistrunk, Michael "Brick" White, Shawn "S.T." Turner, Lil' Rell (Y.G.), Charley Block, Gerald James, Melvin Troy, Tone Ahmed Reid, Lil' Donny, The Bootsey (Collins) brothers, elder Theodore Anwar Moody, Rob Carney, Bumpy Jamal, Ahmed (twin), Stan "Shug" Haines, Rick Alston, Kenyatta, Bro. Ya-Yah, Balagoon, Tim Dockery, Kevin "Black" Bowman, NO-NO, Gary Johnson, Mikey Raw Holmes, Maurice Brock, Toby Aqll Wooten, Taquee, Ya-Yah/Ponch, elder Cetewayo, Andre Amin Robinson, Big Shannon, Jingles/ Akuno (The Moon), Vernon AB Steed, Pretty-Boy Dex, Tone Moton, Lil' Mike/Miguel, Tone/Toot, Khalif, Capt. Keasy, Rashan Brooks-Bey, Sacrifice, Rasheed, Juan Ruiz, Tone Bundy, Ishango Bundy, Alphonso Heru Pugh, and the many others who have been burled

iii

alive in Pennsylvania's invisible HELL-HOLE; whose identities have been hidden behind prison-numbers and statistical mumbo-jumbo, I SEE Y'ALL!

TO THOSE WHO TRANSITIONED while in state captivity: Big 'Preme, Farrakhan (Charley Brown), Old-Head Rock, Charles X Beasley, Big Amin Jabbar, Willie 30X Clayton, Bus-Head, Abdullah Shah, Big Ted X Brown (Champ), Riley "Lil' Cricket" Freeman, J-Rock, Ishmael, and the many others - WE WILL NEVER FORGET!!!

In Solidarity,

Asafo - Unchained

UHURU SASA

(FREEDOM NOW)!

Blessings to the readers of this material.

If you would like to contribute to a

special cause of humanity now you can!

Contact us, purchase this booklet

then share humanity with others.

Nanhill925@gmail.com

1986

2016

RECOMMENDED READING

BLACK-ON-BLACK VIOLENCE
BY DR. AMOS N. WILSON

THE NEW JIM CROW
BY MICHELLE ALEXANDER

THE ASSASSINATION OF THE BLACK MALE IMAGE
BY EARL OFARI HUTCHENSON

THE CONDEMNATION OF BLACKNESS
BY KHALIL GIBRAN MUHAMMAD

MAROON THE IMPLACABLE
BY RUSSELL MAROON SHOATZ

DEFYING THE TOMB
BY KEVIN RASHID JOHNSON

BLACK LIVES MATTER SPEECH
BY KIANGA-YAMAHTTA TAYLOR
20 JANUARY 2016, ALTERNATIVE RADIO

LET THE CIPHER OF SILENCE BE UNBROKEN
BY ASAFO CHUMA ASAFO

THE WRETCHED OF THE EARTH
BY FRANZ FANON

ASAFO: A WARRIOR's GUIDE TO AFRIKAN MANHOOD
BY MWALIMU BOMANI BARUTI

"A day may come - it will come, if
his prayer is heard - a terrible day
of vengeance ... when the master in
his turn will cry in vain for mercy."

- SOLOMON NORTHUP, 12 YEARS A SLAVE

UNITED STATES CONSTITUTION AMENDMENT XIII [1865]

Section 1. Neither slavery nor involuntary servitude, except as a punishment for crime whereof the party shall have been duly convicted, shall exist within the United States, or any place subject to their jurisdiction.

Section 2. Congress shall have power to enforce this article by appropriate legislation.